PARABLES

stories that Jesus told

© 1984 Rourke Publications, Inc.

Published by Geoffrey Butcher 1983

Published by Rourke Publications, Inc., P.O. Box 3328,
Vero Beach, Florida 32964. Copyright © 1984 by Rourke
Publications, Inc. All copyrights reserved. No part of this
book may be reproduced in any form without written per-
mission from the publisher. Printed in the United States
of America.

Library of Congress Cataloging in Publication Data

Butcher, Geoffrey.
    Parables : stories that Jesus told.

    (A Little Shepherd Book)
    Summary: Brief versions of several of the parables
that Jesus told to clarify His lessons.
    1. Jesus Christ—Parables—Juvenile literature.
[1. Jesus Christ—Parables.   2. Parables.   3. Bible
stories—N.T.]   I. Title.   II. Series.
BT376.B88   1984   226'.809505   84-9849
ISBN 0-86625-251-7

PARABLES

stories that Jesus told

Written and illustrated by
GEOFFREY BUTCHER

EAU CLAIRE DISTRICT LIBRARY

Rourke Publications, Inc.
A Little Shepherd Book
Vero Beach, FL 32964

Jesus would often tell stories to help His followers understand the lessons He taught.

One day, they climbed a mountain. There He told His disciples this story.

"People who listen to me and do as I say are like a man who built his house on a rock."

"When the storms and floods came the rock was strong. The house did not fall."

"Those who do not do as I say are like the man who built his house on sand."

"When the storms and floods, came the sand was washed away. The house fell down."

Jesus told them to love their neighbors. One lawyer asked who was his neighbor.

Jesus told of a traveller who was beaten and robbed and left lying by the road.

A priest saw him lying there
and crossed to the other side
of the road.

A temple worker also passed.
Then, a foreigner from Samaria
stopped to help.

The Samaritan bandaged him and took him to an inn. There, he put him to bed.

He paid for the traveller to stay at the inn until he was well again.

Jesus said that this good Samaritan was a true neighbor. The lawyer should be like him.

Priests asked why Jesus talked with sinners. This is one of the stories He told.

A younger son asked for his share of his father's wealth. Then, he left home.

He travelled to a far country.
There, he soon used up all of
his money.

Now, he was so poor and hungry. He had to care for pigs to make money.

He knew that his father's servants were well fed. So, he went home to ask for a job.

His father saw him coming and rushed out to welcome him home.

The boy was sorry for being a bad son. He asked if he could be a servant instead.

The father said no. He had new
clothes brought. A great meal
was prepared. His father was so
happy!

The older son was jealous. He was told that one day all his father's property would belong to him.

The family was happy because the brother they thought was lost had come home.

God is also happy when a sinner who is sorry returns to Him.

Jesus said that the Kingdom of Heaven is like a net that catches all kinds of fish.

The fishermen put the good fish into baskets and throw the bad fish away.

Jesus said that in the same way
God will save good people and
punish the wicked.

Questions to help you understand

1. Why did Jesus tell parables?
2. What happened to the traveller who had been beaten?
3. Who helped him?
4. What was the story about the boy who left home?
5. What does the story mean to you?